THE
YOGI
BOOK

THE YOGI BOOK

"I Really Didn't Say Everything I Said!"

BY Yogi Berra

WORKMAN PUBLISHING · NEW YORK

Library of Congress Cataloging-in-Publication Data is available.

ISBN 978-0-7611-5443-3

Front cover and title page photo: Archive Photos
Back cover photos: Berra Family Collection, Archive Photos

Workman books are available at special discounts when purchased in
bulk for premiums and sales promotions as well as for fund-raising or
educational use. Special editions or book excerpts also can be created
to specification. For details, contact the Special Sales Director at the
address below or send an e-mail to specialsales@workman.com.

Workman Publishing Company, Inc.
225 Varick Street
New York, NY 10014-4381
www.workman.com

Manufactured in the United States of America

First printing February 2010

10 9 8 7 6 5 4 3 2 1

DEDICATION

To my brothers, John (1), Mike (2), and Tony (3), and my sister, Josie (4),
who convinced my parents, Pietro (5) and Paulina (6), to let me leave
home and try to earn a living playing baseball.

To my sons, Larry, Tim, and Dale, and to the rest of the family for
listening and remembering the sayings that I don't even know I say.

To my daughter-in-law Betsy, without whose efforts
this book wouldn't have happened.

And finally, to my beautiful wife, Carmen, who tolerates me
and for whom my love is unending.

From Ralph Terry
pitcher and teammate

When I was a young pitcher I'd have a lead, a man or two on base, no big threat, and Casey Stengel would come to the mound and take me out of the game, after three or four innings. You need five innings in the game to get a win, but I would be gone before. One day Yogi said to me, "Would you like to stay in the game longer?" Sure I would, I said. "When the old man comes out," Yogi said, "don't open the conversation, don't say you feel fine. Don't say anything."

The next time I pitch I have a couple of men on base and Stengel comes out, I don't say anything. Boyer, Richardson

come over, the umpire walks toward the mound, I'm not saying anything. Then Stengel asks, "How do you feel?" I answer, "Fine." Stengel says, "Curve this guy," and he walks away. After that, I never say a word. Yogi knew. He knew Stengel didn't want to be talked into anything, that if he listened and left me in and the next guy hits a home run, he looks bad. Yogi knew him like a kid knows his parents. That's the greatest tip that Yogi ever game me.

Ralph Terry after shutting out the San Francisco Giants, 1–0 in Game 7, to win the 1962 World Series for the Yankees.

From Bob Turley
pitcher and teammate

Yogi and I go way back. He's from St. Louis and I'm from East St. Louis. Thank heavens I had him on my team, because you couldn't strike him out. I played with him eight years on the Yankees. When I was pitching, I'd get to the ninth inning and I'd want to strike the last guy out so Yogi would have the ball and give it to me. I would write on the ball the team and the score, how many strike outs in the game, how many hits, and I'd put the ball on my wall. Most of the other guys on the club would just give me the ball after the last out, but not Yogi. It got to the point where he would not give me the ball unless I gave him two brand-new balls. I asked him why wouldn't he just give it to me, and he said it was his and it was valuable. So I had to give him two new ones.

Yogi and Bob Turley, who pitched in four games of the 1958 World Series against the Milwaukee Braves. The Yankees won in seven games.

From Tony Kubek
Yankee teammate

Do any in this "younger generation" even remember Lawrence Peter Berra as a ballplayer? The man we all called Yogi was a ballplayer's ballplayer; it's the highest tribute his teammates and peer group could give.

Let me take you around the bases with Yogi. If you were on first with Yogi at bat and the first baseman was holding you close, be alive. Yogi saw that open hole between the first and second basemen and he would invariably pull the ball through it. Usually it led to runners at the corners, or, if he got it in the air, it was an HR into Yankee Stadium's right-field stands. You had to be alive, because if you weren't, you might find a lump on your shinbone from a Yogi line drive.

When you reached second base, Yogi was a treat to watch hit. His eyes got bigger. He saw another RBI. Now most teams tried to outfox Yogi and pitch him away, especially in the Stadium, as he was pretty much a dead-pull hitter. That is, unless he decided to go to left field with no one on and two strikes on him. So, they pitched him way, way inside on the first pitch to make him pull the ball foul—strike one. Sometimes they did it twice—strike two. Then, they'd go way, way outside to get him to swing at a bad pitch. Unfortunately for them, Yogi, with those long arms and strong hands, had really outfoxed the opposing catcher's pitch calling and location and set them up to get *his* outside pitch, sometimes six inches out of the strike zone and hittable only by him. Yogi was a great two-strike hitter. As one of his managers, Casey Stengel, the Ole Perfesser, used to say, "You can look it up."

When you were on third base, getting to step on home plate to score a run was as certain as the sun coming up in the morning, with Yogi in the batter's box. Seldom, in this situation, did this renowned "bad ball" hitter swing at a bad pitch. He thrived on hitting with runners in scoring position. His focus was single-minded; get the runner home.

Being at the plate with Yogi on second base was advantageous to a batter. If you were a power hitter like Mickey Mantle, Roger Maris, "Moose" Skowron, or Ellie Howard, Yogi could read the catcher's signals and subtly relay the pitch to them, which gave them a distinct edge. He was a savvy ballplayer.

Yogi's baserunning instincts, his ability to get down in the dirt to block pitches, his uncanny knack of catching foul tips, going after foul balls and getting out of his crouch to field bunts in front of home plate, even into his mid-thirties, well . . . he was one of a kind. When he played in the outfield, he was still an asset. How many catchers have there been who got into and out of their crouch from behind home plate as many times as Yogi and, yet, retained their running speed, agility, and desire to stay back there to take the beating from all of the foul balls, collisions, and second guessing as he did?

So now he's remembered, principally, as an author, a philanthropist for the Yogi Berra Museum and Learning Center, the host of a golf tournament, a regular at Yankee games, a mentor to the younger players, an advisor/consultant to the "Boss," etc., etc.

I've read some of *Bartlett's Familiar Quotations* and Benjamin Franklin's *Poor Richard's Almanac*. On a scale of 10, I give each of them an 8. To Yogi's tome I award 10 points, based on its deeper philosophical meaning, originality, onomatopoeia, alliteration, and clever use of witticisms. I never met the two dudes to whom I gave 8's, but I do know this; they weren't as humble, nor were they as nice a guy as Yogi.

Mr. Berra, do I get a cut on the proceeds?

From Dave Anderson
sports columnist for *The New York Times*

Yogi Berra doesn't hit home runs or catch no-hitters anymore, but as an American folk hero, he's more influential than ever.

If you were to call 973-655-2377, you would hear his familiar voice: "Hi, this is Yogi. Get your pencils ready. This message won't be over until it's done." Then a voice says, "Thanks, Yogi, and thank you for calling the Yogi Berra Museum and Learning Center on the campus of Montclair State University. For hours and admissions, press 1. For directions, press 2. For . . ."

And for Yogi himself, just go to the unpretentious stucco building in Little Falls, N.J., where he'll be talking to some of the 20,000 school kids that arrive in buses each year for a guided tour, or he'll be welcoming famous sports personalities to seminars on sociological topics, or he'll be just hanging out among a captivating collection of baseball memorabilia and sporting exhibits.

You never know when you might hear a new Yogi-ism. When he was wished a happy 80th birthday in 2005, he replied, "I don't want to know how old I am. I want to go backwards"—meaning he wanted to turn 79 a year later, then 78 the year after that. Life doesn't work that way, of course. Not even Yogi's life.

Whatever his age, his nonprofit Museum and Learning Center has embellished his legacy. Opened in 1998, its interactive seminars include: "Your Kid and Sports: What Every Parent Should Know," "Beyond the X's and O's," "The Pre-Game

Show: Preparing for a Winning Career in the Sports Business Industry."

How ironic that Yogi is involved in a "learning center." He disliked school so much in his hometown of St. Louis that he quit after the eighth grade to work in a Pepsi-Cola bottling plant and at a shoe company before joining the Navy during World War II, but in later years he acknowledged that from what his three sons told him, he might have enjoyed college, that archaeology and some psychology courses interested him.

Without realizing it, he had been a psychologist as a Yankee catcher. Instead of scolding a pitcher for lacking the usual velocity on his fastball, he would ask, "Is that as hard as you can throw?" The next pitch hummed.

Despite Yogi's lack of formal education, he learned to never stop learning—about baseball, of course. About what opposing pitchers were throwing. About what pitches to call as a catcher. But also about how to serve on a Navy rocket ship off Normandy on D-day. About how to be himself, how to work hard, how to be a father and a husband, how to be a good family man, how to connect to business opportunities, how to create a spotless reputation. How, quite simply, to live his life.

And perhaps more than anything else, Yogi Berra learned how to help youngsters learn how to live their lives.

From Joe Garagiola
catcher, sportscaster, friend

My friend Yogi Berra and I began sharing our dreams when he was Lawdie and I was Joey, and we were just two baseball-playing youngsters growing up in the Italian-American section of St. Louis that was called "The Hill." These many years later, I'm asked if I'm surprised by all that Yogi went on to accomplish as a major league ballplayer, manager, and coach. I always answer no. Since we were kids, Yogi has been one of the most

The arrow on the left is pointing to Joe; the one on the right is pointing to Yogi.

positive thinkers I have ever known and he's always been successful at everything that has interested him.

Yogi played in a record 14 World Series for the New York Yankees from 1947 to 1963; was voted the American League's Most Valuable Player in 1951, 1954, and 1955; ended his playing career with the most homers by a catcher in major league history; managed the

Yankees to an American League pennant in 1964 and the New York Mets to a National League pennant in 1973; and was elected to the Hall of Fame in 1972. He had a remarkable career. Yet it's funny that his lasting fame has come less from how he played and managed than from his unique way of speaking. Yogi is one of the most quoted people in the world.

Fans have labeled Yogi Berra "Mr. Malaprop," but I don't think that's accurate. He doesn't use the wrong words. He just puts words together in ways nobody else would ever do. You may laugh and shake your head when Yogi says something strange like, "It ain't over till it's over," but soon you realize that what he said actually makes perfect sense. And you find yourself using his words yourself because they are, after all, the perfect way to express a particular idea.

In fact, the key to Yogi-isms is Yogi's simple logic. He may take a different avenue than you would to get to where he's going, but it's the fastest, truest route. What you would say in a paragraph, he says in a sentence. If you say it in a sentence, Yogi needs only one word. If you use one word, Yogi just nods. Yogi's conversation is normal dialogue after-taxes.

I've gotten lost more than once going to Yogi's house in New Jersey, so now I call for directions. Each time, I get a memorable response. A favorite is, "I know just where you are, Joey. You're not too far. But don't go the other way, come this way." Now, I've been accused of putting words in Yogi's mouth, but how could I make up a response like that? How can you improve on Yogi?

From Tim McCarver
catcher and sportscaster

Joe Garagiola says there is one word that comes to mind when he thinks of how people have regarded his lifelong friend Yogi Berra through all the years. *Underestimation.* I agree that's the most salient word that can be said about Yogi. He has been underestimated in many ways during his eventful life, and it's to his everlasting credit that he has turned the tables on all those who misjudged him.

I would imagine that everybody in baseball underestimated Yogi at one time or another, particularly pitchers for a lot of years before they realized how dangerous a hitter he was—and then they still couldn't do anything about it. Ted Williams, perhaps the best hitter ever, played against Yogi's celebrated Yankee teammates Joe DiMaggio and Mickey Mantle, yet called Yogi the game's best clutch hitter—that's pretty high praise. Underestimating his physical skills was the first mistake his opponents made. Yogi stood only 5'8" and didn't have the build of any other successful player in history, but he was agile behind the plate and had built-in power and the uncanny ability to hit balls in the dirt or in the clouds. Underestimating his intelligence was the second mistake.

You may think this is odd, but when I recently read a biography of Abraham Lincoln I thought of Yogi Berra. To me, Yogi as a player was almost like Lincoln as a politician. Lincoln was tall and gaunt, the opposite of Yogi, but his intelligence and leadership skills were as underestimated for a time. There were many politicians who had more presence than Lincoln, but when he opened his mouth and delivered oratory, people were agog at how much sense he made. Whenever Yogi, who has always been as modest and self-deprecating as our sixteenth president, took center stage, greatness came out, too.

Like Lincoln, Berra never underestimated himself. He, too, felt there was no need to boast, he just accepted how good he was. Talk about two men being very comfortable in their own skins. Lincoln stood above everyone else, appearing out of nowhere in a century in which no one for decades before him or after him was at all like him. That's how it was with Yogi Berra, a one-of-a-kind ballplayer. Lincoln became president and experienced immediate duress when he was thrown right into a war. A former outfielder, Berra was forced to learn the catching job under fire while the Yankees fought for the pennant. Brilliance, guts, and talent succeeded in both instances.

I have no problem using the word *brilliance* in regard to Yogi Berra. For years I didn't fully understand or appreciate the nature of Yogi's wisdom, inside baseball (as a player, manager, or coach) or outside. Like everyone else, I was taken by his whimsy and laughed with amusement at the oft-quoted Yogi-isms in this book. But when Yogi said one of his gems, any instinct to mock him was immediately trumped by an inclination to say, "Wait a minute, if you consider that line from this perspective and that perspective, it actually makes good sense." It can't be said of many people that their wisdom is represented by their non sequiturs. In fact, Yogi is the only one. I don't believe for one second that it was chance that has led him to such good fortune in his own life, overcoming low expectations by others and as many obstacles as Lincoln did. It was wisdom. So I would advise that if Professor Berra says anything, even something that sounds a bit cockeyed, file it away until the next time you come to a fork in the road.

From Billy Crystal
lifelong Yankees fan

I would like to thank Yogi for making this book necessary. Yogi Berra is a national treasure. He is an ambassador during a special time in our lives, a human bridge to our childhoods when all we really cared about was a Yankee win, a Mantle home run, and beating the Dodgers in October. He was dependable, he was clutch, and because of that he was respected, and he was feared. Now all these years later, he is loved. He is cherished because he has never really changed. He is still the most caring, honest, decent, and good-humored player and person of his generation. His statistics will always stand, but to know Yogi is to know the charming, humorous, and caring man he really is. I'm proud to say I know him that way, and now with this book, I hope you'll feel you know him, too.

Comic, actor, author, and devout
Yankee fan, Billy Crystal.

INTRODUCTION

To the Most Quoted Man
from Larry, Tim & Dale Berra

I f we had a penny for every time we were asked what it was like to grow up with Yogi Berra as our father, we would probably own the world's largest pile of copper. It's certainly easy to recall the lineup of memorable events that most kids wouldn't have had the opportunity to experience: the times we played catch with Elston Howard in front of the dugout at Yankee Stadium; or got dunked in the clubhouse whirlpool by Mickey Mantle; or got patted on the head by Casey Stengel, as if we were favorite pets. But when we tell people about growing up as Yogi's sons, we always make it clear that to us everything seemed normal, even trips to the ballpark. That normalcy was a reflection of Dad.

So many times we have heard how difficult it was for someone growing up as the son or daughter of a celebrity. They had a tough time because the pressure was too great to live up to his or her legacy. As Yogi's sons, we never had that problem because our dad never acted like he was a celebrity. We have a famous father who prefers driving a Corvair to a Cadillac because it's more practical. Who treats the man who pumps his gas or sells him his newspaper as a good friend. And who makes the bed before leaving the house in the morning. It doesn't take much to make Dad happy. He finds joy in playing with his grandchildren, watching a good movie, or sinking a putt.

Because our father likes to keep life from becoming too complicated, he has made it an art to get to the root of any problem in about five seconds. Faced with the most complex equation, he will trim off the fat and, we marvel, come up with the easiest yet most profound—and quotable— solution imaginable. That he is able to do this is a gift. The three of us just haven't figured out what this gift is. No one has.

Left to right: Tim, Larry, and Dale.

The person who might have the best idea is our mom, Carmen Berra, and she's not saying. Next to every great man is a great woman, and such is the case with Yogi and Carmen. Mom is intelligent and beautiful, as well as insightful. She had to be. How else could she have fallen for Dad? She knew what she was doing because they've been happily together for nearly fifty years. However, only Dad is responsible for Yogi-isms.

Another favorite question asked of us is whether Dad really said all those great lines that have been attributed to him. We don't know the sources of the numerous bogus Yogi-isms that are floating around, but we can tell you that the quotes included in this book are the real deal. Authentic Yogi Berra. Arlene Francis once asked Dad if he had read a biography someone had written about him and he replied, "Why should I? I was there." Well, we were there for Dad's classic Yogi-isms (and will be there for the future ones, too). We hope you enjoy them as much as we do!

"I really didn't say everything I said!"

This was a comment I made when someone asked me about quotes that I didn't think I said. Then again, I might have said 'em, but you never know.

Making speeches isn't for me. I'd rather the audience just asked me questions.

"Thank you for making this day necessary."

I think this was the saying that got it all started. Yogi Berra Day, 1947. I was being honored by my friends on The Hill in St. Louis.

Here I am with the Stags, the first team I played on as a kid. In the back (left to right) are Joe Garagiola, me, and Ben Pucci. Kneeling (left to right) are Charlie Riva and Johnny Columbo. This was taken at the Missouri Hall of Fame.

"You can't think and hit at the same time."

I could always see bad balls good. This ball looks like it saw me, too. At the time, I was a coach for the Yankees and knocking grounders to the infield before a game with Cleveland.

If you ask me, this is true with any sport. I said it in 1946 when I was with the Newark Bears playing Triple A. My manager told me not to swing at balls out of the strike zone. He said, "Yogi, next time you're up, think about what you're doing." I struck out in three pitches!

A writer asked me, "What makes a good manager?" I answered: **"Good players!"**

A few of the best came to a preseason reunion in St. Petersburg. That's me with Eddie Lopat, Roger Maris, Casey Stengel, and Hank Bauer.

Whitey Ford says:

I've heard all the Yogi stories and have been involved in some, but when I think of Yogi, I realize there's so much to him—he has a great family, he's so honest, and helps his friends any way he can. The only bad thing I can say about Yogi is he never bought me a beer!

Me and my buddy Whitey.

"Nobody goes there anymore. It's too crowded."

I was maître d' at Ruggeri's for a couple of years in the '40s, during the off-season. At that time, both Joe Garagiola and my brother John were waiters.

I was talking to Stan Musial and Joe Garagiola in 1959 about Ruggeri's restaurant in my old neighborhood in St. Louis. It was true!

"A nickel ain't worth a dime anymore."

Who would doubt this? I notice it especially when I go to buy my papers in the morning at Henry's in Verona, New Jersey.

In 1955, I did an opening for a snack bar in the Bronx. Despite what it looks like in this photo, I wasn't the only one to enjoy ice cream that day.

SERVICE

ICE CREAM DISHES

Cone or Cup 10¢
Large Cone or Cup 20¢
Floats 25¢
Sundaes 30¢
Thick Shakes 30¢
Pints 45¢
Banana Home Run 45¢
Quarts 85¢

SNACKS

Doughnut 5¢
Frankfurter 15¢
French Fries 15¢
Hamburger 25¢

No glove, see what
happens—I got hit
with a pitched ball
during the 1952
World Series and
broke my thumb.

"The only reason I need these gloves is 'cause of my hands."

This is a doozie. Carm, Tim, and I were in the backyard gardening. I began complaining about getting scratches and mud all over my hands. Carmen really let me have it. She finally threw me a pair of gloves, and this was my reply.

Me: "Where have you been?"

Carmen: "I took Tim to see *Doctor Zhivago*."

Me: "What the hell's wrong with him now?"

Our game got rained out and I got home early. I was hungry.

When Tim played football for the University of Massachusetts in the early '70s, Carm and I used to go up every chance we got.

Nolan Ryan is soaking
his fingers in pickle juice
pregame—he said it pre-
vented blisters! With him
are Phil Linz and Kenny
Boswell (with his head in
the basket).

"We were overwhelming underdogs."

I was reminiscing with Nolan Ryan one day about the 1969 Amazing Mets.

Nolan Ryan says:

If Yogi had gone to college, they would have made him talk clearer, but not better.

"The other teams trouble for us if

Here we are before the opener of the 1952 World Series against the Dodgers (from left to right): Johnny Mize, Joe Collins, Gene Woodling, Gil McDougald, Hank Bauer, Phil Rizzuto, Billy Martin, Irv Noren, me, and Mickey Mantle. It doesn't get much better than this!

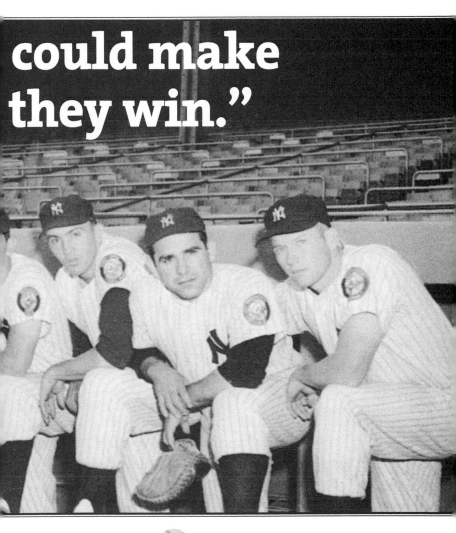

could make they win."

 Well, if they lose, they're no trouble at all.

"It's never happened in World Series history, and it hasn't happened since."

I was referring to the 1956 perfect game pitched by Don Larsen.

This was the most exciting game I ever caught. Nobody talked about it in the dugout, not even Don and I. We couldn't—we were ahead by only two runs. I didn't know I was going to jump on Don until I jumped on him.

"It's déjà vu all over again."

My comment after Mickey Mantle and Roger Maris hit back-to-back home runs for the umpteenth time. Makes perfect sense to me.

This picture was taken at a baseball clinic that was held in an armory in Manhattan. Gil Hodges, Phil Rizzuto, and Eddie Lopat were also there the day this photo was shot.

When asked the time, I replied: **"You mean now?"** I don't know when I first said this, but for some reason it stuck with me and I say it all the time!

Here I am, clearing out my locker. My son Larry was obviously no help!

"We made too many wrong mistakes."

I said this after the 1960 World Series between the Yankees and Pirates. It was a seven-game series that ended when Bill Mazeroski hit the doggone home run over my head. There was no other way to explain how we ever lost that Series.

As you can see by my face, we were in trouble!

"If people don't want to come to the ballpark, how are you going to stop them?"

Yes, I said this. I was talking to commissioner Bud Selig when attendance was down around the league. I think it was due to the threat of a strike.

Another close play for me at home plate. I'm putting the tag on Phillies shortstop Granny Hamner in the final game of the 1950 World Series.

It was 1964, I was managing the Yankees, and the season opener with the Red Sox was one day away. I must have said something of note 'cause that guy on the left looks like he's trying to figure out how to interpret it.

"If you ask me a question I don't know, I'm not going to answer."

After a rough game, any questions seem like tough ones. Sometimes you just don't feel like talking about it. But like it or not, you have to face the press. So, after a difficult loss, I announced this to the writers before they had a chance to ask me a question.

"Slump? I ain't in no slump . . . I just ain't hitting."

I never, ever thought I was in a slump. As far as I was concerned, tomorrow I was always going to get my hits, regardless of what I did today.

I'm swinging away here! Hope it was a good one.

"It was hard to have a conversation with anyone, there were too many people talking."

I was at the White House for dinner by invitation of President Ford. Those politicians were so noisy, I couldn't hear a thing.

Gerald R. Ford says:

I was involved with a very special golf event in Vail, Colorado, for twenty years—The Jerry Ford Invitational. I recall one year on the thirteenth hole of the Vail Golf Club, Yogi's pants split. In perhaps what was the greatest nonverbal "Yogi-ism," the crowd roared when they realized he actually had on Yogi Bear undershorts.

I beat Julius Erving in a shoot-out at Beaver Creek, Colorado. He wasn't happy. Here, President Ford is giving me a congratulatory handshake.

Playing golf one day,
I started to complain that my
shot was going to go into the
water. My friend Kevin Carroll
said, "Come on, Yogi, don't be like
that. Think positively." I replied:
**"Okay, I'm positive my shot
is going into the water."**

I recognize that look on my
face. It's the one I get when a
drive isn't headed where I'd
like it to go. This time it was
during an American Airlines
Golf Classic. Hey, at least I
have on a great outfit.

"90% of short putts don't go in."

 So all right, they never go in!

I often practiced my putting in the living room. Larry and Tim should have paid more attention!

"Why buy good luggage? You only use it when you travel."

 My teammates were always ribbing me about my old luggage. You couldn't hurt my bags, but theirs could only get worse.

That's Larry having a good time watching Carmen help me pack, back in the early days. Or should I say both of us were watching Carmen do the packing?

"When you come to a fork in the road, take it."

I was giving Joe Garagiola directions from New York to our house in Montclair when I said this. Another time I was giving Joe directions and I told him, "I know just where you are. Don't go the other way, come this way." Joey has known me almost all my life. He always finds me.

The Stags, when we were The Stags, the first team I played for growing up in St. Louis. In the back (left to right): Ben Pucci, Andrew (I forget his last name—we called him Nah Nah), and Charles (our sponsor—he paid for our shirts). In the middle (left to right): Bob Berra (no relation), Charlie Riva, me, and Paul Agusti. Sitting in front (left to right): Joe Garagiola, George di Philippo, Pete Fansani, and Aldo Rossi.

"We're lost, but we're making good time!"

I was voted into the Hall of Fame in 1972 and it was the greatest! Here I am on the big day in Cooperstown, New York. With me and my plaque are Joe Garagiola and Ed Stack, president of the Hall of Fame.

I said this on the way to the Hall of Fame in Cooperstown in 1972. My wife, Carmen, and my sons, Larry, Tim, and Dale, were all in the car. Hard to believe it, but I got lost. Carmen was giving me a hard time, so I gave it back.

"If the world were perfect, it wouldn't be."

I believe you have to take the good with the bad, otherwise how do you know when things are good? If the world were perfect, how would you know?

The umpire called me out on strikes here. I guess I was a little upset.

I was receiving the key to New York City on a miserably hot and humid day. Mayor Lindsay's wife, Mary, commented on how cool I looked, and I replied: **"You don't look so hot yourself."**

I guess I was a little nervous about the speech I had to make.

See? I was in style way back when.

During an interview, Bryant Gumbel told me he wanted to do some word association. The first thing he said was: "Mickey Mantle." I replied: **"What about him?"**

Mickey and me on
Opening Day in 1956.

Phil Rizzuto says:

Of all the Yogi Berra stories I know (and I know quite a few), there is one that is my favorite. Yogi and Carmen invited my wife, Cora, and me to see their new home in Montclair, New Jersey. After having a tour, my reaction was: "Wow, Yogi! What a beautiful mansion you've got here!" Yogi replied: "What do you mean, Phil? It's nothing but a bunch of rooms."

Phil Rizzuto and I played a lot of cards when we traveled. Phil was a great shortstop, but a lousy card player.

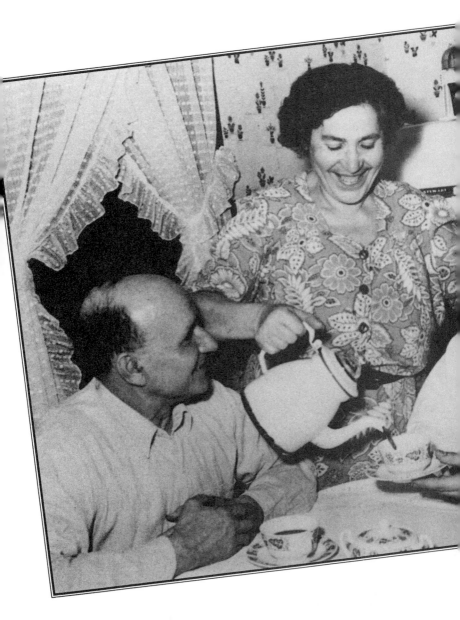

A reporter asked me, "What would you do if you found a million dollars?" I replied: **"I'd see if I could find the guy that lost it, and if he was poor, I'd give it back."**

My parents always taught me to be honest. I figured if someone lost that much money, he'd be broke.

Me with my father, Pietro, and mother, Paulina. My mom made great coffee. Really strong. It would grow hair on your chest.

"If I didn't wake up I'd still be sleeping."

I had set my alarm and it didn't go off. Man, was I relieved that I woke up on time.

This was taken during a barnstorming trip to Japan in the 1950s. At the end of the season, the Japanese invited players from the U.S. to compete against their teams. We had a ball.

Carmen and I were on our way back from one of our trips to Japan. I guess my nap was out of the question.

"I usually take a two-hour nap from 1 to 4."

Life on the road could get kind of crazy, so it helped me to have a routine. All of my career, I would wake up, eat breakfast, go for a walk, come back and read the paper, have a little lunch, and then take my two-hour nap—from 1 to 4.

"If you can't imitate him, don't copy him."

I said this when I was with the New York Mets. During batting practice one day, I was leaning up against the cage and overheard Ron Swoboda saying that he wanted to hit like the great Hall of Famer Frank Robinson. Ron was trying to stand up close to the plate like only Frank could do, daring you to throw it in on him.

Just me being a ham.

"It gets late early out there."

Left field in Yankee Stadium was tough to play during the late autumn. World Series time! The shadows would creep up on you and you had a tough time seeing the ball off the bat. Everyone knew what I meant . . . I think.

Me and Yankee Stadium right before my managerial debut in the 1964 opener with Boston.

 I was asked, "Yogi, when you were young, what did you like best about school?" I answered: **"When it's closed."**

I've been asked that question a lot, and I always give the same answer. I guess I drove the teachers crazy when I was a kid. I begged my mom and pop for years to let me quit and go to work. In those days, things were different. I wanted to work and help my family.

This was taken during a 1942 American Legion game in Hastings, Nebraska. That's Gene Mauch on the right, catching.

"90% of the game is half mental."

I have said this many times. It's one of my better coaching tips.

I'm giving good advice, I hope, at a Little League clinic that was held at Yankee Stadium.

While playing a game of twenty questions, I asked: **"Is he living?" "Is he living now?"**

People still rib me about this one. We used to play twenty questions or cards to pass the time on train trips. This particular time, I was playing with Del Webb, then part owner of the Yankees.

Just a bunch of us killing time on the train. Standing (left to right): Joe Page, Eddie Lopat, and Ralph Houk. Sitting (left to right): Tommy Henrich, me, Allie Reynolds, and Sherm Lollar.

"Always go to other people's funerals, otherwise they won't go to yours."

Mickey and I had been talking about all the funerals we'd been to in that one year. We were saying that pretty soon there would be no one left to come to ours.

Maybe Mickey and I were pointing this out to restaurateur Toots Shor during one of our many visits to our favorite night spot.

Carm and I with the
boys and our cocker
spaniel, Taffy.

"Steve McQueen looks good in this movie. He must have made it before he died."

After Christmas dinner, Carmen, Larry, Tim, Dale, and I were sitting in the den watching *Papillon*. Come on now—I was half asleep—you know what I meant.

"I'm as red as a sheet."

You may not know that I appeared in the movie *That Touch of Mink* with Cary Grant and Doris Day. You'd think I'd be used to embarrassing moments after playing big-league games in front of so many people. But after flubbing my line during the movie shoot, I flubbed the apology, too.

My movie debut, with Doris Day and Cary Grant no less. That's Roger Maris and Mickey Mantle on either side of Doris. I'm next to Cary.

I was a movie critic for a while and was asked if the movie *Fatal Attraction* had frightened me. I remarked: **"Only the scary parts."**

This was the logo used when I was a movie critic. It was drawn by Tom Villante, who used to be a batboy for the Yankees.

After seeing the opera *Tosca*, Carmen and I were on our way back to the hotel. She asked me what I thought and I replied: **"I really liked it. Even the music was good."**

Carmen has never let me live this one down.

I'm dishing out my special spaghetti at a sports celebrity luncheon held in Los Angeles as a charity fund-raiser.

When asked if I wanted my pizza cut into four or eight slices, I replied: **"Four. I don't think I can eat eight."**

Roger Maris, Mickey Mantle, and me on the bus to somewhere. Probably on the way to a meal. We always went out to eat together. Get a load of Mickey's hat!

"I wish I had an answer to that, because I'm tired of answering that question."

The Yankees weren't doing well and day after day I was asked why. I truly didn't have an answer, but I sure wish I did. When I came up with this reply, all the reporters said, "You said one again, Yogi!"

It must have been a good
day. Look at that smile.

We were shooting the breeze in the clubhouse when the subject of having insurance came up. My response was: **"I don't know what the best type is, but I know none is bad."**

Most people I know still argue which kind to buy.

This shot of me with my son Larry was definitely set up. I didn't change diapers. Well, occasionally, but only when they were wet.

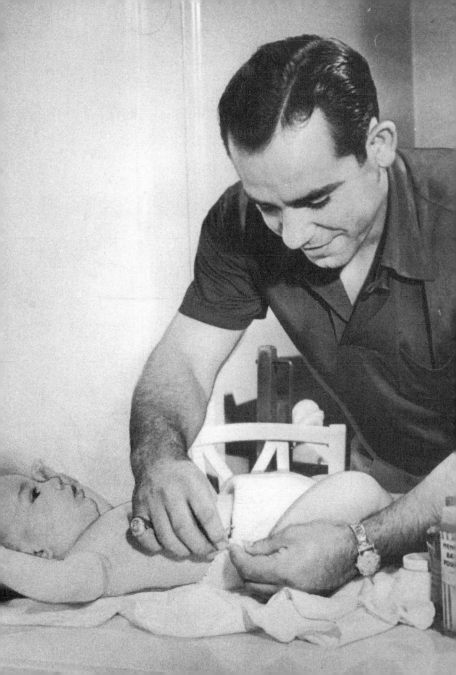

When Max Nicholas, then head of Yankee public relations, called, I sleepily answered the phone. "Sorry, Yogi," he said. "I hope I didn't wake you." I replied: **"Nah, I had to get up to answer the phone anyway."**

This photo was taken in my office at the bowling alley that Phil Rizzuto and I owned from the late '50s to the mid '60s. It was a landmark on Route 3 in New Jersey, just west of New York City.

At a Yoo-Hoo convention, a woman asked me, "Is Yoo-Hoo hyphenated?" I responded: **"No ma'am, it isn't even carbonated!"** I thought she was referring to the ingredients.

From the early '50s to the '60s, I worked for Yoo-Hoo and enjoyed sampling the goods.

Dale and me after he was acquired by the Yankees from the Pirates. He was the first major leaguer to play full-time on a team managed by his father. I'm a very proud papa.

"Pair up in threes."

During spring training at the Ft. Lauderdale stadium, I was making the players do wind sprints after a tough loss. I was looking at Dave Righetti, Bob Shirley, and my son Dale when I said this.

After doing a radio show with Jack Buck in St. Louis, a check was handed to me made out to "Pay to Bearer." I turned to Jack and said: **"You've known me all this time and you still can't spell my name!"**

Jack Buck at the mike, calling a Cardinals game.

With Johnny Bench catching, it was no wonder we lost to the Reds four straight in 1976.

"Congratulations. I knew the record would stand until it was broken."

I sent this in a telegram to Johnny Bench after he broke my record for most home runs by a catcher.

"Don't get me right, I'm just asking!"

I was negotiating a new contract with Yankees owner Dan Topping. We didn't have agents back then and I didn't want to insult him.

Here I am in 1963 signing on to manage the Yankees. With me are general manager Ralph Houk (left) and co-owner Dan Topping (standing).

"Never answer an anonymous letter."

This isn't as bad as it sounds. Some letters do have return addresses with no name, you know.

I think the expression on my face says it all. I couldn't have been more pleased than when I signed my contract to become the Yankees' manager in 1963.

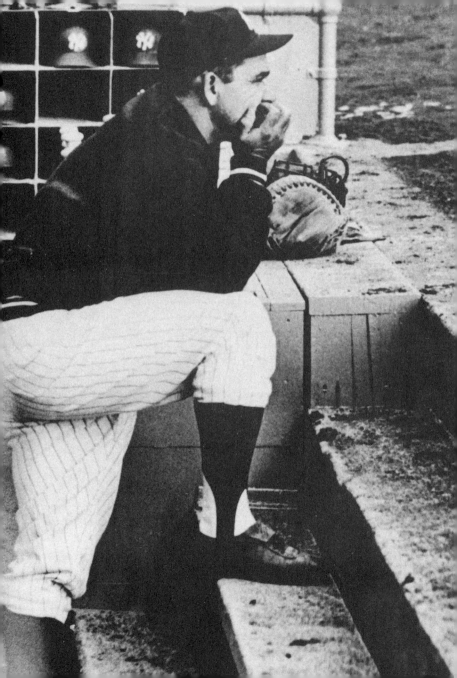

"You can observe a lot by watching."

I was managing the Yankees in 1964 when I said this. I yelled it to the players, who were not paying attention to the game.

Managing is very stressful, sometimes downright nerve-racking. Here I am in an obvious nail-biter.

 My roommate Bobby Brown was studying to become a doctor. I was well known for my avid comic book reading. One night, Bobby looked up from reading his anatomy textbook and asked me how my comic book turned out. I said: **"Great, and how did yours come out?"**

My good buddies Bobby Brown and Tommy Byrne (the toughest pitcher I ever caught) during the 1952 World Series against the Dodgers.

My favorite pastime back then.

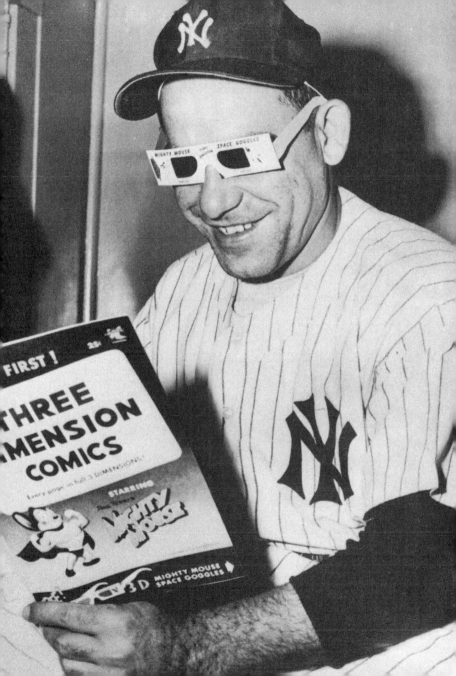

Don Mattingly says:

What sticks in my mind the most is Yogi's comment about all the batting practice I used to take. "Don," he said, "you're going to hit yourself right into a slump."

 When I was managing the New York Yankees, a reporter asked if Don Mattingly had exceeded his expectations this season. I replied: **"I'd say he's done more than that."**

The day this photo was taken in 1984, Don got four hits in a game against the Detroit Tigers. One of my favorite people, Don ended the year with a .343 batting average and the AL batting championship.

"It's not too far, it just seems like it is."

I am the absolute worst at directions, or so I'm told. I was trying to tell someone how to get to our old racquetball club.

Taking in the sights in Japan on one of our off-season barnstorming trips.

When I was told that a Jewish mayor was elected in Dublin, Ireland, I responded: **"Only in America!"**

What can I say? Geography was never my strong point.

Here I am signing my quota of balls for the day.

"You've got to be careful if you don't know where you're going 'cause you might not get there."

If you don't set goals, you can't regret not reaching them.

I'm not sure it was my goal to wind up with three sons, but here I am with my third, Dale.

When a reporter asked me if Joe DiMaggio was fast, I answered: **"No, he just got there in time."**

Joe and I were in the clubhouse celebrating our 1951 World Series win.

During an interview, Arlene Francis asked me if I had read my new book, *Yogi: It Ain't Over* .... I said: **"No, I was there."** Well, I was.

Casey Stengel and me in 1972 at the New York Press Photographers annual sports awards dinner.

When asked, "Yogi, what size cap do you want?" I replied: **"I don't know. I'm not in shape yet."**

Every spring we would get fitted for new uniforms. It's a big ordeal and pretty boring. Once in a while, I can come up with a joke. This one I'm still hearing about.

This was taken at my home in the winter. I'm really not in shape yet—can't seem to get to my toes!

When I returned home from Italy, Cardinal Spellman asked me if I had had an audience with the Pope. I said, "No, but I saw him." Then I was asked what I had said to His Holiness. I couldn't remember exactly, but he said, "Hello, Yogi," and I responded: **"Hello, Pope."**

Cardinal Spellman is presenting me with the Christian Youth Organization award.

When I was coaching with the Houston Astros, Marc Hill, Gene Clines, and I were on our way to play golf. I was in the backseat of the car, and all at once it started to rain. I asked: **"Where's that coming from?"**

Those two wanted to call the networks to tell them what I had said!

Looking up, but I doubt that I have the weather on my mind.

We were going to have some of our blinds repaired, only I didn't know it. I was upstairs when my son Larry called out, "Dad, the guy is here for the venetian blinds." I told him: **"Look in my pants pocket and give him five bucks."**

My kids would take turns coming to games with me and sitting in the dugout. Here Larry joins me during a Mets game.

In the dugout, someone said to me, "Yogi, you're ugly," and I said: **"So? I don't hit with my face."**

Razzing and ribbing takes place all the time in baseball. The visiting team dugouts really gave it to me, so I had to give it back.

I look like Hannibal Lecter here.

While speaking with writers before the 1973 playoffs about the Cincinnati "Big Red Machine," I said: **"Tony Perez is a big clog in their machine."**

Here's Tony at bat in 1973, at Shea Stadium. Although I never got to play against him, I had a lot of opportunities to watch him play. He's a nice guy and was a helluva clutch hitter.

"We have a good time together, even when we're not together."

This just slipped out when someone asked me about my beautiful wife.

Me and Carm cutting a rug at Grossinger's, a one-time popular resort in the Catskills.

"Little League baseball is a good thing 'cause it keeps the parents off the streets and the kids out of the house!"

Maybe this should be the other way around. All kidding aside, I do think Little League can be a great experience for kids, but it should be fun!

I was giving the Pinehurst Lions Club team a few pointers here.

"The future ain't what it used to be."

I just meant that times are different. Not necessarily better or worse. Just different.

Mickey Mantle, me, Whitey Ford, Joe DiMaggio, and Casey Stengel got together at Yankee Stadium before an Old Timers game in 1974.

Buddy Harrelson was called out trying to score in the tenth inning of the
second game of the 1973 World Series.
As good an umpire as Augie Donatelli
was, he got this one wrong—and I let
him know it!

"It ain't over till it's over."

That was my answer to a reporter when I was managing the New York Mets in July 1973. We were about nine games out of first place. We went on to win the division.

1925

May 12
Lawrence Peter "Yogi" Berra born in St. Louis.

1939

Goes from playing barefoot sandlot ball to joining American Legion team.

1942

Cardinals slight Yogi and instead sign best friend Joe Garagiola, who lived across the street on Elizabeth Avenue in St. Louis.

1943

Yankees sign Yogi to contract. Assigned to Norfolk farm club in Piedmont League.

1944–1945

Serves in Navy, sailing for the British Isles on the USS *Bayfield*.

1944
June 6
Participates in D-day invasion as Gunner's Mate.

1946
September 22
Debut with Yankees. Hits two-run homer.

1947
September 30
First World Series game. Goes on to set records for most Series played (14) and championships (10).

1947
October 2
Hits first pinch-hit homer in World Series history, against Dodgers.

1949
January 26
Marries Carmen.

1949

July 12
Plays in first of 15
All-Star Games.

1949

December 8
Laurence A. (Larry) Berra born.

1951

September 23
Son Tim born. Later played wide receiver
for Baltimore Colts.

1951

September 28
Catches Allie Reynolds' second no-hitter
of season.

1951

November 8
Wins first of three AL MVP Awards. Also
wins in 1954 and 1955. Received MVP
votes for 15 consecutive seasons.

1955

Leads Yankees in RBIs
for seventh consecutive
season.

1956

October 8
Catches Don Larsen's
perfect game in Game 5
of World Series.

1956

October 10
Hits two HRs in 9–0 win over
Dodgers in Game 7 of Series.

1956

December 13
Son Dale born. Later played 11
seasons in majors with Pirates,
Yankees, and Astros.

1959

September 19
Yogi Berra Day at Yankee
Stadium.

1962

June 24
Catches all 22 innings
of game vs. Detroit,
at age 37.

Ted Williams, left, and
Joe DiMaggio, center.

1963

October 24
Retires as player. Named
manager of Yankees.

1964

August 22
Slaps harmonica out of hands
of Phil Linz, who refuses to stop
playing instrument on team bus.

1964
October 3
Yankees clinch AL
pennant in his first
year as manager.
Celebrates with
Pedro Ramos.

1964
October 17
In hometown of St.
Louis, Yankees lose Game 7
of World Series to Cardinals.

1964
October 23
Yankees fire Yogi as
manager.

1964
November 17
Hired as player-coach for
New York Mets.

1965

May 9
Last major league at bat,
three days before his 40th
birthday. Lifetime, Yogi had
7,555 at bats.

1969

With Berra as
coach under
manager Gil
Hodges, Mets
stun baseball
world by
winning World
Series.

1972

January 19
Elected to Hall of Fame.

1972

April 2
Becomes manager of
Mets after Gil Hodges
dies of heart attack.

Yogi with Bowie Kuhn.

1972

July 22
Yankees retire
Yogi's number, 8.

1973

October 2
After being in
last place in late
August, leads Mets to NL East
championship with 82–79 record.

1973

October 10
Mets win NL pennant by upsetting Reds
in Championship Series.

1973

October 20
Mets lose World Series to Oakland A's in
seven games.

1975

August 6
Mets fire Berra as manager.

1976

Rejoins Yankees as a coach. Team plays
in four World Series in his eight seasons
as coach.

1983

December 6
Hired as manager of Yankees, to begin in
1984 season.

1985

April 10
Dale Berra plays third base for Yankees
with Yogi as manager.

1985

April 28

Yankees fire Berra as manager with club holding 6–11 record. Begins 14-year feud with Steinbrenner. Refuses to go to Yankee Stadium until 1999.

1986

Hired as coach of Houston Astros.

1988

August 22

Given plaque in Monument Park in Yankee Stadium. Refuses to attend because of feud with Steinbrenner.

1989

September 26

Retires as coach of Astros.

1999

April 9
Yogi Berra sets foot in
Yankee Stadium for the
first time in 14 years.
Throws out the first
pitch on Opening Day.

1999

July 18
On Yogi Berra Day,
catches ceremonial
first pitch from Don
Larsen. David Cone
then pitches perfect
game vs. Expos.

2009
October 28
Flanked by Michelle Obama
and Jill Biden, throws out
ceremonial first pitch before
first game of World Series at
new Yankee Stadium.

Putting it all together:
Words of inspiration from Yogi

This is an excerpt from the commencement speech I delivered when I received my honorary doctorate from Montclair State University in 1996.

Just call me
Dr. Berra.

A lot of people have been quoting me ever since I came to play for the Yankees in 1946. But, as I once said, I really didn't say everything I said. So now it's my turn. I want to give some of my famous advice to the graduates.

First: Never give up, because it ain't over till it's over.

Second: During the years ahead, when you come to a fork in the road, take it.

Third: Don't always follow the crowd, because nobody goes there anymore. It's too crowded.

Fourth: Stay alert—you can observe a lot by watching.

Fifth and last: Remember that whatever you do in life, 90 percent of it is half mental.

In closing, I want to quote myself again: Thank you, Montclair State University, for making this day necessary.

My pride and joy— they made this book necessary.

2.

4.

5.

3.

6.

Yogi

1.

7.

13.

9.

8.

14.

10.

15.

11.

12.

Apples Don't Fall Far From The Tree

1. Carmen: "I need to go shopping for clothes to shop in."

2. Larry: "You can't lose if you win."

3. Tim: "I knew exactly where it was, I just couldn't find it."

4. Dale: "The similarities between my father and me are different."

5. Betsy: "Sometimes you have to get lost to find yourself."

6. Carla: "I'm so hungry right now, I can't even look at food."

7. Lindsay: "The water is cold until you get wet."

8. Larry Jr.: "This is very poorly unorganized."

9. Gretchen: "Grammy has so many clothes, she never wears the same outfit once."

10. Bridgette: "Shut up and talk."

11. Whitney: "How can I find it if it's lost?"

12. Christopher: "I eat apples, but not fruit."

13. Andrew: "I don't remember leaving, so I guess we didn't go."

14. Maria: "I double-checked it six times."

15. Nicholas: "I'm hiding these right here!"

PHOTO CREDITS

Page 5: Daily News, L.P. New York

Page 6: Associated Press

Page 7: Time & Life Pictures/Getty Images

Page 12: National Baseball Library & Archive Photo Collection

Page 17: Getty Images

Page 19: Berra Family Collection

Page 20: AP/Wide World Photos

Page 23: Sporting News/ Archive Photos

Page 24: AP/Wide World Photos

Pages 26–27: AP/Wide World Photos

Pages 28–29: Cleveland Press/Everett Collection

Page 30: UPI/Corbis-Bettmann

Page 33: AP/Wide World Photos

Page 34: AP/Wide World Photos

Page 37: Berra Family Collection

Page 38: UPI/Corbis-Bettmann

Pages 40–41: AP/Wide World Photos

Page 43: AP/Wide World Photos

Page 44: Daily News, L.P.

Page 47: Berra Family Collection

Page 48: Berra Family Collection

Pages 50–51: AP/Wide World Photos

Page 52: AP/Wide World Photos

Page 55: Everett Collection

Page 57: Berra Family Collection

Page 58: Cleveland Press/ Everett Collection

Page 61: Bob Olen/Berra Family Collection

Page 62: Bob Gilman/Berra Family Collection

Page 65: Sporting News/ Archive Photos

Page 66: Berra Family Collection

Page 69: AP/Wide World Photos

Pages 70–71: Berra Family Collection

Page 73: AP/Wide World Photos

Page 74: Daily Mirror/Corbis

Page 76: National Baseball Library & Archive Photo Collection/Bettmann Archive

Page 79: National Baseball Library & Archive Photo Collection/Bettmann Archive

Page 81: National Baseball Library & Archive Photo Collection/Bettmann Archive

Page 83: Archive Photos

Page 84: Daily News, L.P. New York

Pages 86–87: Sporting News/Archive Photos

Page 88: National Baseball Library & Archive Photo Collection

Pages 90–91: UPI/Corbis-Bettmann

Page 93: Bill Mark/Berra Family Collection

Page 94: National Baseball Library & Archive Photo Collection

Page 98: Tom Villante Marketing Inc.

Page 101: Berra Family Collection